CHRISTMAS AT HOME

Cookie
Lover's
COOKBOOK
HOLIDAY RECIPES
& MORE

MariLee Parrish

© 2008 by Barbour Publishing, Inc.

Compiled by MariLee Parrish.

ISBN 978-1-60260-159-8

Published by Barbour Publishing, Inc., P.O. Box 719, Uhrichsville, Ohio 44683, www.barbourbooks.com

Our mission is to publish and distribute inspirational products offering exceptional value and biblical encouragement to the masses.

Printed in China.

A special thank you and many Christmas blessings to JoAnne and Mom and all my friends and family who sent me recipes for this book: Jeannie Berry, Kristy Peatrowsky, Miriam Ramsey, and Connie Krizon.

I thank my God every time I remember you.
PHILIPPIANS 1:3

Contents

Old-Fashioned Favorites

I heard the bells on Christmas Day
Their old familiar carols play,
And wild and sweet the words repeat
Of peace on earth, goodwill to men!

HENRY WADSWORTH LONGFELLOW

Jake's Banana Cookies

1 cup sugar
1 cup butter
2 eggs
½ cup sour cream
1 cup mashed bananas

4 cups flour
2 teaspoons baking powder
1 teaspoon baking soda
½ teaspoon salt

Mix all ingredients. Bake at 350 degrees for 12 to 15 minutes.

Frosting:
1 (8 ounce) package cream cheese
½ cup butter

1 teaspoon vanilla
1 pound powdered sugar

Cream in order, frost cookies, and decorate with Christmas sprinkles.

Old-Fashioned Peanut Butter Cookies

2½ cups flour
1 teaspoon baking powder
1 teaspoon baking soda
¼ teaspoon salt
1 cup butter

1 cup peanut butter
1 cup sugar
1 cup brown sugar
2 eggs
1 teaspoon vanilla

Stir flour, baking powder, baking soda, and salt and set aside. Beat butter and peanut butter until smooth. Beat in sugars, eggs, and vanilla. Add flour mixture. Chill dough if necessary. Shape into 1-inch balls and place on ungreased cookie sheet. Bake at 350 degrees for 12 minutes. Makes 6 dozen.

Oatmeal Scotchies

¾ cup butter, softened
¾ cup sugar
¾ cup brown sugar
2 eggs
1 teaspoon vanilla
1½ cups flour

1 teaspoon baking soda
1 teaspoon cinnamon
½ teaspoon salt
3 cups rolled oats
2 cups butterscotch chips

Preheat oven to 375 degrees. Beat butter and sugars together. Add eggs and vanilla, beating well. Stir together dry ingredients with whisk until well blended. Gradually add to creamy mixture and stir until blended. Stir in oats and butterscotch chips. Drop spoonfuls onto ungreased cookie sheet. Bake for 7 to 9 minutes or until edges begin to brown. Store in sealed container. Makes about 4 dozen.

*Happy, happy Christmas, that can win us back
to the delusions of our childhood days, recall to the old man the
pleasures of his youth, and transport the traveler
back to his own fireside and quiet home!*

CHARLES DICKENS

Jeanne's Oatmeal Cookies

1 cup packed brown sugar
½ cup sugar
¾ cup shortening
1 egg
¼ cup water

1 teaspoon vanilla
3 cups quick oats
1 cup flour
1 teaspoon salt
½ teaspoon baking soda

Preheat oven to 350 degrees. In large bowl, beat sugars and shortening until creamy. Add egg, water, and vanilla; beat well. Add combined oats, flour, salt, and baking soda; mix well. Drop dough by rounded teaspoons onto ungreased cookie sheet. Bake for 11 to 13 minutes or until edges are golden brown. Remove to wire rack. Cool completely. Store tightly covered. Makes about 5 dozen.

Old-Fashioned Snickerdoodles

½ cup butter or margarine
¾ cup sugar
1 medium egg
1 teaspoon baking powder

¼ teaspoon salt
1⅔ cups flour
2½ tablespoons sugar mixed
   with 1½ teaspoons
   cinnamon

Preheat oven to 400 degrees. Combine margarine and sugar in large bowl. Add egg and beat until creamy. Add baking powder, salt, and flour. Stir until mixture forms thick dough. Put cinnamon-sugar mixture in small bowl. Shape dough into 1-inch balls. Roll in cinnamon-sugar mixture. Place on greased cookie sheet. Using bottom of cup, press balls to flatten slightly. Bake for 10 minutes.

Perfect Pumpkin Cookies

2½ cups flour
1 teaspoon baking powder
1 teaspoon baking soda
½ teaspoon salt
2 teaspoons cinnamon
½ teaspoon nutmeg

¼ teaspoon cloves
½ cup butter, softened
1 cup brown sugar
1 can pumpkin puree
1 egg
1 teaspoon vanilla

Icing:

2 cups powdered sugar
3 tablespoons milk

1 tablespoon butter
1 teaspoon vanilla

Chocolate Drop Cookies

½ cup shortening
2 squares unsweetened baking chocolate
2 eggs
1 cup sugar
½ teaspoon vanilla
1⅓ cups flour

Preheat oven to 400 degrees. Melt shortening and chocolate together in medium saucepan. Remove from heat. Beat eggs; add sugar and whisk together well. Add melted chocolate mixture, vanilla, and flour. Mix well. Drop by heaping tablespoons onto ungreased cookie sheet. Bake for 6 minutes.

Mom's Gingersnaps

¾ cup shortening
1 cup brown sugar
¼ cup molasses
1 egg
2¼ cups flour
2 teaspoons baking soda

½ teaspoon salt
1 teaspoon ginger
1 teaspoon cinnamon
½ teaspoon cloves
Granulated sugar

Preheat oven to 350 degrees. Cream shortening, brown sugar, molasses, and egg until fluffy. Sift together flour, baking soda, salt, and spices. Stir into molasses mixture. Form into small balls. Roll in granulated sugar. Place 2 inches apart on greased cookie sheet. Bake for 10 minutes. Do not overbake, or cookies will be too hard.

Old-Fashioned Walnut Balls

1 cup butter
⅓ cup brown sugar
1 teaspoon vanilla
2 cups flour
½ teaspoon salt
1½ cups finely chopped walnuts
Powdered sugar

Preheat oven to 375 degrees. Cream butter, brown sugar, and vanilla until fluffy. Sift flour and salt together; add to creamed mixture. Mix well; stir in walnuts. Shape dough into walnut-sized balls. Bake on ungreased cookie sheet for 12 to 15 minutes. Remove from cookie sheet. When still warm but cool enough to handle, roll in powdered sugar. Makes about 4 dozen.

Poppy Seed Cookies

½ cup vegetable oil
1½ cups sugar
2 eggs
1 teaspoon vanilla

¼ cup milk
½ cup poppy seeds
4 cups flour
2 teaspoons baking powder

Preheat oven to 350 degrees. Mix oil and sugar. Add eggs, vanilla, and milk. Mix well. Add poppy seeds. Add flour and baking powder and mix lightly until smooth. Break off piece of dough. Roll out on floured surface and cut out shapes with cookie cutters. Bake on ungreased cookie sheet for 12 minutes or until edges are golden.

Old-Fashioned Molasses Cookies

3 cups flour
2 teaspoons baking soda
1 teaspoon salt
1 teaspoon ginger
1 teaspoon cinnamon
¾ cup evaporated milk

¾ tablespoon cider vinegar
1 cup shortening
1 cup sugar
1 egg
½ cup molasses

Preheat oven to 375 degrees. Stir together flour, baking soda, salt, and spices. Combine evaporated milk and vinegar. Cream shortening and sugar thoroughly; add egg and molasses. Beat well. Add evaporated milk and vinegar alternately with dry ingredients. Mix well. Drop spoonfuls onto greased cookie sheet. Bake for about 10 minutes. Watch carefully to avoid overbaking. Remove from pan to cool.

Gingerbread Cookies

6 cups flour
1 tablespoon baking powder
1 tablespoon ginger
1 teaspoon nutmeg
1 teaspoon cinnamon
½ teaspoon cloves

1 cup shortening, melted
1 cup molasses
1 cup packed brown sugar
½ cup water
1 egg
1 teaspoon vanilla

Sift together flour, baking powder, ginger, nutmeg, cinnamon, and cloves. Mix shortening, molasses, brown sugar, water, egg, and vanilla until smooth. Gradually stir in dry ingredients. Divide dough into 3 pieces, wrap in plastic wrap, and refrigerate for at least 3 hours. Preheat oven to 350 degrees. On lightly floured surface, roll dough to ¼-inch thickness. Cut with cookie cutters. Place 1 inch apart on ungreased cookie sheet. Bake for 10 to 12 minutes.

Cream Cheese Cutouts

1 cup butter, softened
1 (8 ounce) package cream cheese,
  softened
1½ cups sugar

1 egg
1 teaspoon vanilla
3½ cups flour
1 teaspoon baking powder

In large bowl, beat butter and cream cheese until well combined. Add sugar; beat until fluffy. Add egg and vanilla; beat well. Combine flour and baking powder. Add dry ingredients to cream cheese mixture; mix well. Divide dough in half. Wrap each portion in plastic wrap; refrigerate for about 2 hours. Preheat oven to 375 degrees. On floured surface, roll dough to ⅛-inch thickness. Cut with cookie cutters. Place 2 inches apart on ungreased cookie sheets. Bake for 8 to 10 minutes or until edges are lightly browned. Remove to wire racks to cool completely. Makes about 7 dozen.

Old-Fashioned Preserve Thumbprints

1 (8 ounce) package cream cheese, softened
¾ cup butter, softened
1 cup powdered sugar
2¼ cups flour

½ teaspoon baking soda
½ cup chopped pecans
½ teaspoon vanilla
Strawberry and peach preserves

Beat cream cheese, butter, and powdered sugar until smooth. Add flour and baking soda; mix well. Add pecans and vanilla; mix well. Chill dough for at least 30 minutes. Preheat oven to 350 degrees. Shape dough into 1-inch balls. Place on ungreased cookie sheet. Press thumb in middle of each cookie; fill with about 1 teaspoon preserves. Bake for 14 to 16 minutes or until light golden brown. Cool on wire rack. Makes about 3 dozen.

Old-Fashioned Sugar Cookies

½ cup butter
1 cup sugar
½ teaspoon vanilla
   or other flavoring
2 eggs
2 cups flour

2 teaspoons baking powder
¼ teaspoon salt
1 tablespoon milk
Additional sugar

Preheat oven to 350 degrees. Cream butter with sugar; add vanilla and eggs. Mix thoroughly. Sift flour and baking powder with salt and add to egg mixture. Add milk and mix well. Add additional flour if needed for consistency to roll. Break off small pieces of dough; roll on floured surface and sprinkle with sugar. Dip cutter in flour and cut out cookies. Bake on lightly greased cookie sheets for about 10 minutes. Allow to cool before decorating.

Sour Cream Drops

2 sticks butter
2 cups sugar
3 eggs
1 teaspoon vanilla
1 cup sour cream
4 cups flour
1 teaspoon baking powder
½ teaspoon baking soda
¼ teaspoon salt

Frosting:
4 tablespoons butter
1 cup powdered sugar
½ teaspoon vanilla
6 to 8 teaspoons hot water

Cream butter and sugar. Mix in remaining ingredients. Chill for 1 to 2 hours. Drop by teaspoons on greased cookie sheet. Bake at 350 degrees for 10 to 12 minutes or until light brown. **Frosting:** Melt butter in saucepan until golden brown. Stir in powdered sugar, vanilla, and enough water to achieve spreading consistency. Frost cooled cookies and decorate with Christmas sprinkles or colored sugar.

Sour Cream Cutouts

2 eggs
1½ cups sugar
1 cup butter, softened
¾ cup sour cream
1 teaspoon vanilla

4 cups flour
1 teaspoon baking powder
1 teaspoons baking soda
½ teaspoon salt

Cream eggs, sugar, butter, and sour cream. Add remaining ingredients. Mix well and chill for at least 2 hours. Roll out on lightly floured surface and cut with cookie cutters. Bake at 375 degrees for 10 minutes.

sort of sharp

Great-Grandma's Lemon Sugar Cookies

3 cups flour
2 teaspoons baking powder
½ teaspoon salt
2 cups sugar

1 cup shortening
2 eggs
¼ cup lemon juice
Additional sugar

Stir together flour, baking powder, and salt; set aside. In large mixing bowl, beat sugar and shortening until fluffy; beat in eggs. Stir in dry ingredients. Add lemon juice. Mix well. Chill for at least 2 hours. Preheat oven to 350 degrees. Shape into balls and roll in sugar. Place on greased baking sheets 2 inches apart; flatten with fork. Bake for 8 to 10 minutes or until lightly browned.

5 dz.

Fancy and Fun

Awake, glad heart! get up and sing!
It is the birthday of thy King.

HENRY VAUGHAN

Chocolate Truffles

⅔ cup heavy whipping cream
2 cups semisweet or milk
  chocolate chips
2 teaspoons vanilla

Coating:
  Cocoa
  Flaked coconut
  Toffee bits
  Chopped nuts
  Christmas sprinkles

In saucepan, heat cream almost to a boil. Remove from heat and add chocolate chips. Whisk gently until chocolate is melted and mixture is smooth. Stir in vanilla and pour into bowl. Cover and refrigerate for 3 hours or until firm. **Coating:** When chocolate mixture is firm, scoop into 1-inch balls and roll in your favorite coatings. Cover and refrigerate for 2 hours. Serve cold. Keep refrigerated in airtight container. Makes approximately 30 truffles.

Almond Toffee Cookies

4½ cups flour
1 teaspoon baking soda
1 teaspoon cream of tartar
1 teaspoon salt
2 sticks salted butter, softened
1 cup vegetable oil
1 cup sugar

1 cup powdered sugar
2 eggs
1 teaspoon almond extract
2 cups sliced almonds,
toasted and chopped
1 (10 ounce) package English
toffee bits

Preheat oven to 350 degrees. Whisk together flour, baking soda, cream of tartar, and salt. Cream butter for 30 seconds. Beat in vegetable oil and sugars. Add eggs one at a time, beating well after each addition. Beat in almond extract. Gradually add flour mixture to creamed mixture. Mix until just combined. Stir in almonds and toffee bits. Drop by teaspoons on ungreased cookie sheets. Bake for 10 to 12 minutes. Remove from cookie sheet immediately. Makes 9 dozen.

Lemon Pistachio Cutouts

2¼ cups flour
3 teaspoons baking powder
½ teaspoon salt
1 stick salted butter, softened

1 cup sugar
1 egg
1 tablespoon half-and-half
1 teaspoon lemon extract

Egg wash:
2 egg yolks

1 teaspoon water

Topping:
⅓ cup sugar
1¼ cup finely chopped pistachios

½ teaspoon lemon zest

Whisk together flour, baking powder, and salt. Cream butter and sugar. Beat in egg, half-and-half, and lemon extract. Gradually add flour mixture to creamed mixture. Mix well. Cover and refrigerate for 2 hours. Preheat oven to 350 degrees.

Egg wash: Beat egg yolks and 1 teaspoon water; set aside.

Topping: Combine sugar, pistachios, and lemon zest. On lightly floured surface, roll out dough to ⅛-inch thickness. Cut with floured cookie cutter. Place 1 inch apart on ungreased cookie sheets. Brush tops of cookies with egg wash; sprinkle with pistachio mixture.

Bake for 6 to 8 minutes. Do not overbake. Remove from cookie sheet immediately. Makes 4 dozen.

Chocolate Caramel Cookies

3 cups flour
½ cup cocoa
3 sticks salted butter, softened
1 cup sugar
1 egg
1 teaspoon vanilla
1 (12 ounce) package semisweet
   chocolate chips
1 cup finely chopped pecans, toasted
1 bottle caramel ice cream topping

Chocolate drizzle:
½ cup semisweet
   chocolate chips, melted
2 teaspoons butter
   or margarine

Preheat oven to 350 degrees. Whisk together flour and cocoa. Cream butter and sugar. Beat in egg and vanilla. Gradually add flour mixture. Stir in chocolate chips and pecans. Roll into 1-inch balls and place on ungreased cookie sheet. Press thumb in center of each ball. Fill each indentation half full with caramel topping. Bake for 15 to 18 minutes. Let cookies set for 5 minutes before removing from cookie sheet. **Chocolate drizzle:** In microwave-safe bowl, melt chocolate chips and shortening on medium-high for 1 to 2 minutes. Stir until smooth. With fork, drizzle chocolate over cookies. Makes about 5 dozen.

White Chocolate Raspberry Cookies

8 ounces white chocolate chips, divided
½ cup butter, softened
1 cup sugar
1 teaspoon baking soda
¼ teaspoon salt
2 large eggs
2¾ cups flour

Topping:
½ cup seedless raspberry jam
3 ounces white chocolate chips
½ teaspoon shortening

Preheat oven to 375 degrees. Lightly grease large cookie sheet. In large measuring cup, melt 4 ounces white chocolate chips in microwave on high for 30 seconds. Stir. Repeat until chips are melted and creamy. Beat butter on medium-high speed for 30 seconds. Add sugar, baking soda, and salt. Beat until combined. Beat in eggs and melted white chocolate chips until combined. Beat in flour a little at a time. Stir in remaining unmelted white chocolate chips. Drop by teaspoons onto prepared cookie sheet. Bake for 7 to 9 minutes. Let cookies set for 1 minute before removing from pan. **Topping:** Just before serving, warm jam in microwave. Spoon about ½ teaspoon jam on each cookie. Melt 3 ounces white chocolate chips and ½ teaspoon shortening in microwave on high for 30 seconds. Stir. Repeat until chips are melted and creamy. With fork, drizzle white chocolate over cookies. Let stand until set. Makes 4 dozen.

White Chocolate Macadamia Nut Cookies

2 cups flour
1 teaspoon baking soda
1 teaspoon cream of tartar
½ teaspoon salt
1 stick salted butter, softened
½ cup shortening
½ cup sugar

½ cup packed brown sugar
1 egg
1 teaspoon vanilla
6 ounces white chocolate chips
½ cup coarsely chopped
   macadamia nuts, toasted
Additional sugar

Combine flour, baking soda, cream of tartar, and salt. Cream butter, shortening, sugars, egg, and vanilla. Gradually add flour mixture. Stir in white chocolate chips and nuts. Refrigerate for 1 hour. Preheat oven to 400 degrees. Shape dough into 1-inch balls and roll in sugar. Place on ungreased cookie sheet; flatten slightly. Bake for 8 to 10 minutes. Remove from cookie sheet immediately. Makes about 5 dozen cookies.

Turtle Cookies

2½ cups pecan halves
½ cup water
¾ cup salted butter, softened
½ cup sugar
1 teaspoon vanilla

1 egg
1½ cups flour
¼ cup cocoa
48 round milk chocolate–
    covered soft caramels,
    unwrapped

Preheat oven to 375 degrees. Soak pecan halves in water while making dough; drain well. Beat butter, sugar, vanilla, and egg until light and fluffy. Beat in flour and cocoa until dough firms. Place 5 pecans in turtle pattern for each cookie on ungreased cookie sheet. Shape dough into 1-inch balls. Place ball on top of each group of 5 pecans, pressing lightly into pecans. Bake for 7 to 10 minutes. Immediately press 1 caramel gently on top of each cookie. Let cookies set for 3 minutes before removing from sheet. Makes 4 dozen.

Key Lime Cookies

1½ cups flour
½ cup powdered sugar
½ cup cornstarch
2 sticks salted butter,
   softened
1½ tablespoons fresh
   key lime juice
1 teaspoon key lime zest

Glaze:
   1¼ cups powdered sugar
   1 teaspoon key lime zest
   2 tablespoons fresh
   key lime juice

Combine flour, powdered sugar, and cornstarch. Beat butter for 30 seconds. Gradually add flour mixture. Stir in key lime juice and zest. Mix until dough forms. On lightly floured surface, shape dough into 2 logs. Wrap each log in plastic wrap; refrigerate for about 2 hours. Preheat oven to 350 degrees. With sharp knife, cut dough into ¼-inch slices. Place on ungreased cookie sheets. Bake for 9 to 11 minutes. Cool for 1 minute before removing from cookie sheet. **Glaze:** Combine powdered sugar and key lime zest. Gradually stir in enough lime juice for desired glazing consistency. Top cookies with glaze. Let set for 15 minutes. Makes 6 dozen.

Peter's Treats

1 cup butter, softened (no substitutions)
1 cup powdered sugar
1 teaspoon vanilla
1¼ cups flour
1 cup quick oats
Dash salt
Chocolate star candies

Cream butter, powdered sugar, and vanilla. Stir in flour, oats, and salt. Shape dough into 2 rolls. Wrap and seal in waxed paper. Chill for at least 2 hours. Preheat oven to 350 degrees. Cut dough into ¼-inch slices and place on ungreased cookie sheets. Top each with chocolate star. Bake for 10 to 12 minutes.

Almond Madeleines

2 large eggs
⅔ cup sugar
1 teaspoon vanilla
½ teaspoon lemon zest
Pinch salt

1 cup flour
1¼ sticks unsalted butter,
    melted, cooled slightly
Powdered sugar, raspberries,
    and whipped cream

Preheat oven to 350 degrees. Butter and flour pan for large madeleines or use mini muffin cups. Beat eggs and sugar in large bowl. Beat in vanilla, lemon zest, and salt. Add flour; beat just until blended. Gradually add melted butter, beating just until blended. Spoon 1 tablespoon batter into each indentation in pan or muffin cup. Bake for 25 to 30 minutes or until lightly browned. Cover and refrigerate for at least 2 hours. Run sharp knife around each cookie and carefully remove from pan. Dust cookies with powdered sugar. Serve with raspberries and whipped cream.

Chocolate-Dipped Almond Crescents

1 cup butter
½ cup sugar
2 teaspoons vanilla
2 teaspoons water
2 cups flour
1 cup chopped almonds
⅔ cup powdered sugar

Chocolate coating:
3 cups candy-coating chocolate
1 tablespoon butter or
   shortening
½ teaspoon almond extract

Cream butter and sugar. Stir in vanilla and water. Add flour and almonds. Mix until well blended. Wrap dough tightly in plastic wrap and chill for at least 3 hours. Preheat oven to 325 degrees. Shape dough into crescents. Place on ungreased cookie sheet and bake for 15 to 20 minutes. Remove from pan to cool on wire racks. When cool, roll in powdered sugar. **Chocolate coating:** Melt chocolate and butter over low heat in heavy saucepan. When melted, add almond extract and stir. Dip one end of cookies into chocolate and place on waxed paper. Place in refrigerator until chocolate is set. Store at room temperature in airtight container.

Bonbon Kisses

1 (12 ounce) package semisweet
 chocolate chips
¼ cup butter
1 (14 ounce) can sweetened
 condensed milk
2 cups flour
1 teaspoon vanilla

30 milk chocolate candy
 kisses
30 chocolate-striped candy
 kisses
2 ounces white chocolate
 chips

Preheat oven to 350 degrees. In medium saucepan, combine semisweet chocolate chips and butter; cook and stir over very low heat until smooth. Add condensed milk; mix well. Combine flour, chocolate mixture, and vanilla; mix well. Shape 1 tablespoon dough around each candy kiss, covering completely. Place on ungreased cookie sheets. Bake at 350 degrees for 6 to 8 minutes. Do not overbake. Remove from cookie sheets and let cool. Melt white chocolate chips in microwave for 30 seconds. Stir. Repeat until smooth and creamy. Drizzle over cookies with fork. Store in covered container. Makes 5 dozen.

Vanilla Pecan Crescents

1 cup powdered sugar, divided
2 sticks butter
¼ teaspoon salt
2 teaspoons vanilla
1½ cups flour
1¼ cups quick oats
½ cup finely chopped pecans

Preheat oven to 325 degrees. Cream ½ cup powdered sugar and butter then add salt and vanilla, blending well. Add flour, oats, and pecans; blend thoroughly. Drop dough by tablespoons onto ungreased cookie sheet. Shape into crescents. Bake for 15 minutes. Remove from cookie sheets and sprinkle remaining powdered sugar over warm cookies.

Pecan Chocolate Chip Tassies

1 cup butter, softened
6 ounces cream cheese, softened
2 cups flour
¼ cup sugar

Filling:
1 pound light brown sugar
3 eggs, beaten
3 tablespoons butter, melted
Dash salt
¼ teaspoon vanilla
½ cup semisweet chocolate
  chips
½ cup chopped pecans

Beat butter and cream cheese until smooth; add flour and sugar, beating until mixture forms smooth dough. Cover; refrigerate about 1 hour or until dough is firm. Shape dough into 1-inch balls and press each ball onto bottom and up sides of small muffin or tart cups to make shells. **Filling:** Slowly beat brown sugar into eggs. Mix in butter, salt, and vanilla. Put spoonful of chocolate chips and ½ teaspoon chopped pecans in each shell; add filling and top with a few more chopped pecans. Bake for 25 minutes at 350 degrees until set. Makes about 4 dozen.

Almond Biscotti

¼ cup finely chopped almonds
½ cup sugar
2 tablespoons margarine
4 egg whites, lightly beaten
2 teaspoons almond extract

Dash cinnamon
2 cups flour
2 teaspoons baking powder
¼ teaspoon salt
Melted chocolate

Preheat oven to 375 degrees. Place almonds in small baking pan. Bake for 7 to 8 minutes or until golden brown (watch carefully to avoid burning). Set aside. Beat sugar and margarine until smooth. Add egg whites, almond extract, and cinnamon; mix well. Combine flour, baking powder, and salt in large bowl; mix well. Stir egg white mixture and almonds into flour mixture until well blended. Spray two loaf pans with cooking spray. Evenly divide dough between prepared pans. Spread dough evenly over bottoms of pans with wet fingertips. Bake for 15 minutes or until knife inserted in center comes out clean. Remove from oven and turn onto cutting board. As soon as loaves are cool enough to handle, cut each into 16 (½-inch thick) slices. Place slices on baking sheets sprayed with cooking spray. Bake for 5 minutes; turn over. Bake for 5 minutes more or until golden brown. Dip in melted chocolate. Cool completely and store in airtight container.

Caramel Nut Thumbprints

4 cups flour
1 teaspoon baking soda
½ teaspoon salt
2½ cups packed brown sugar, divided
1 cup butter or margarine, softened

2 eggs
2 teaspoons vanilla
½ cup sour cream
2 cups finely chopped
    walnuts

Preheat oven to 350 degrees. Combine flour, baking soda, and salt and set aside. Combine 1½ cups brown sugar and butter. Beat until light and fluffy. Add eggs and vanilla. Beat until blended. Add flour mixture and mix well. Shape dough into 1-inch balls. Place on ungreased cookie sheet. Combine remaining 1 cup brown sugar and sour cream in medium bowl and mix well. Stir in walnuts. Press thumb in center of each ball. Spoon 1 teaspoon walnut mixture into each indentation. Bake for 10 to 12 minutes. Cool on cookie sheet for 2 minutes and then remove.

Chocolaty Favorites

Our hearts grow tender with childhood memories and love of kindred,

and we are better throughout the year for having, in spirit,

become a child again at Christmastime.

LAURA INGALLS WILDER

Favorite Chocolate Chip Cookies

⅔ cup shortening
⅔ cup butter (no substitutions)
1 cup sugar
1 cup packed brown sugar
2 eggs
2 teaspoons vanilla

3 cups flour
1 teaspoon baking soda
1 teaspoon salt
1 (12 ounce) package
    semisweet chocolate chips

Preheat oven to 375 degrees. Cream shortening, butter, sugars, eggs, and vanilla. Add flour, baking soda, and salt. Mix in chocolate chips. Drop 1-inch spoonfuls on ungreased cookie sheet and bake for approximately 8 minutes or until golden brown.

Peanut Butter Chocolate Kisses

1 cup butter, softened
1 cup peanut butter
1 cup sugar
1 cup brown sugar
1 (16 ounce) package chocolate
   candy kisses

2 teaspoons vanilla
3½ cups flour
2 teaspoon baking soda
1 teaspoon salt
2 eggs
Additional sugar

Combine butter, peanut butter, and sugars; blend until creamy. Add eggs and vanilla; blend. Mix flour, baking soda, and salt. Add to creamed mixture; mix well. Shape dough into balls and roll in sugar. Bake at 350 degrees for 7 minutes. Place kiss in center of each cookie 2 to 3 minutes after removing from oven.

Kristy's Konsties

2 cups sugar
3 tablespoons cocoa
½ cup margarine
½ cup milk

⅛ teaspoon salt
3 cups quick oats
½ cup peanut butter
1 teaspoon vanilla

In heavy saucepan, bring sugar, cocoa, margarine, milk, and salt to a rapid boil; boil for 1 minute. Add oats, peanut butter, and vanilla; mix well. Working quickly, drop spoonfuls onto waxed paper and let cool.

Chocolate Chip Icebox Cookies

1 cup butter, softened
½ cup sugar
½ cup light brown sugar
2 eggs
1½ teaspoons vanilla

¼ teaspoon salt
3 cups flour
¾ cup finely chopped
    semisweet chocolate chips

Cream butter and sugars; add eggs, vanilla, and salt. Beat until fluffy. Gradually add flour; stir in chocolate chips. Divide dough into 2 logs. Wrap each log in plastic wrap or waxed paper. Refrigerate dough for at least 4 hours or until very firm. Cut into ¼-inch slices and place on greased baking sheet about 1 inch apart. Bake at 350 degrees for 8 to 10 minutes.

Chocolate Whoopie Pie Cookies

1½ cups margarine or butter, softened
3 cups sugar
3 eggs
2 teaspoons vanilla
5½ cups flour

⅔ cup cocoa
1½ teaspoons baking soda
1½ teaspoons salt
2¼ cups buttermilk

Preheat oven to 350 degrees. Cream margarine and sugar. Add eggs and vanilla, beating until fluffy. Sift dry ingredients and add alternately with milk. Chill dough for at least 1 hour. Drop onto greased baking sheet. Bake for 8 minutes. Let cool completely before filling.

Filling:

2 egg whites
2 teaspoons vanilla
¼ cup flour
3 tablespoons milk
2 tablespoons powdered sugar
1 cup shortening
2½ cups powdered sugar

Beat egg whites until stiff. Add vanilla, flour, milk, and 2 tablespoons powdered sugar and mix. Add shortening and 2½ cups powdered sugar, beating until fluffy. Spread between cookies. Keep refrigerated or frozen.

Double Chocolate Cookies

1 (12 ounce) package semisweet
  chocolate chunks
2 cups flour
½ cup cocoa
2 teaspoons baking powder
1 teaspoon salt
10 tablespoons unsalted butter

½ cup sugar
1½ cups packed brown sugar
4 eggs
2 teaspoons instant coffee
  granules
1½ teaspoons vanilla

Melt chocolate in microwave for 30 seconds. Stir. Repeat until smooth. Sift together flour, cocoa, baking powder, and salt. Cream butter with sugars until smooth. Beat in eggs one at a time; then stir in coffee granules and vanilla until well blended. Stir in melted chocolate. Using wooden spoon, stir in dry ingredients just until blended. Cover and let stand for 35 minutes. Preheat oven to 350 degrees. Line 2 cookie sheets with parchment paper. Drop dough by rounded tablespoons onto prepared cookie sheets. Bake for 8 to 10 minutes. Cookies will be set with soft centers. Allow cookies to cool on sheets for 10 minutes before removing.

Rocky Road Cookies

1¼ cups flour
½ cup butter, softened
¼ cup packed brown sugar
1 teaspoon vanilla
½ teaspoon baking soda
¼ teaspoon salt

1 egg
½ cup chopped peanuts
½ cup raisins
½ cup milk chocolate chips
½ cup mini marshmallows

Preheat oven to 375 degrees. Put flour, butter, brown sugar, vanilla, baking soda, salt, and egg into large mixing bowl. Beat until well blended, scraping bowl occasionally. Stir in peanuts, raisins, and chocolate chips. Drop by heaping tablespoons onto greased cookie sheets. Bake for 10 minutes. Remove cookies from oven; press several marshmallows onto each cookie. Bake cookies for 2 minutes more or until marshmallows are slightly melted and sticking to cookies. Remove from sheets to cool completely. Store in tightly covered container for up to 1 week. Makes about 2 dozen.

Chocolate Chip Cream Cheese Drops

½ cup butter or margarine, softened
3 ounces cream cheese
¼ cup sugar
¼ cup packed brown sugar
1 egg

1 teaspoon vanilla
1 cup flour
½ teaspoon salt
1 cup semisweet
    chocolate chips

Preheat oven to 350 degrees. Cream butter, cream cheese, and sugars. Beat in egg and vanilla. Sift together flour and salt; stir into creamed mixture. Stir in chocolate chips. Drop by teaspoons onto lightly greased cookie sheet. Bake for 12 to 15 minutes or until lightly browned around edges. Makes about 3 dozen.

Chocolate Chip Pumpkin Cookies

1 teaspoon baking soda
1 teaspoon milk
1 cup pumpkin
¾ cup sugar
½ cup vegetable oil
1 egg

2 cups flour
2 teaspoons baking powder
1 teaspoon cinnamon
½ teaspoon salt
1 cup semisweet chocolate chips
1 teaspoon vanilla

Preheat oven to 375 degrees. Dissolve baking soda in milk and set aside. Combine pumpkin, sugar, oil, and egg; stir. Add flour, baking powder, cinnamon, salt, and baking soda mixture. Mix well. Stir in chocolate chips and vanilla. Spoon onto cookie sheet. Bake for 10 to 12 minutes. Be careful not to overbake. Cookies will be soft and moist.

Chocolate Chip Peanut Butter Cookies

2¼ cups flour
1 teaspoon baking soda
1 teaspoon salt
¾ cup butter, softened
⅓ cup peanut butter

¾ cup sugar
¾ cup brown sugar
1 teaspoon vanilla
2 eggs
1 cup semisweet chocolate chips

Preheat oven to 350 degrees. Combine flour, baking soda, and salt and set aside. Beat butter, peanut butter, sugars, and vanilla until creamy. Add eggs one at a time, beating well after each addition. Gradually add flour mixture. Stir in chocolate chips. Bake for 11 to 13 minutes.

Chocolate Lace Cookies

⅔ cup butter, melted
2 cups quick oats
1 cup sugar
⅔ cup flour
¼ cup light corn syrup

¼ cup milk
1 teaspoon vanilla
¼ teaspoon salt
2 cups milk chocolate chips

Preheat oven to 375 degrees. Combine butter, oats, sugar, flour, corn syrup, milk, vanilla, and salt; mix well. Drop by teaspoons onto foil-lined cookie sheets. Flatten each cookie until thin with rubber spatula. Bake for 5 to 7 minutes. Let cool. Peel foil away from cookies and let cool. Melt chocolate chips in microwave for 30 seconds. Stir. Repeat until smooth. Spread chocolate on flat side of half the cookies. Top with remaining cookies.

Chocolate Oatmeal Sandwich Cookies

2½ cups plus 2 tablespoons
    butter, softened
1 cup sugar
1½ cups packed brown sugar
2 eggs
4 teaspoons vanilla, divided
2½ cups flour
½ cup cocoa

2 teaspoons baking soda
1 teaspoon salt
6 cups quick oats
1 (12 ounce) package semisweet
    chocolate chips
1 (14 ounce) can sweetened
    condensed milk

Preheat oven to 375 degrees. Beat 2½ cups butter and sugars until fluffy. Beat in eggs and 3 teaspoons vanilla. Combine flour, cocoa, baking soda, and salt. Add to creamed mixture. Stir in oats. Drop by tablespoons onto ungreased cookie sheets. Bake for 10 minutes. Cool. In saucepan, combine chips, condensed milk, 2 tablespoons butter, and 1 teaspoon vanilla. Over medium heat, cook and stir until chips are melted. Immediately spread filling between cooled cookies.

Banana Chocolate Chip Cookies

⅔ cup shortening
1 cup sugar
2 eggs
1 teaspoon vanilla
2¼ cups flour
2 teaspoons baking powder

¼ teaspoon baking soda
½ teaspoon salt
3 small ripe bananas, mashed
1 (12 ounce) package
   milk chocolate chips

Preheat oven to 400 degrees. Blend shortening and sugar. Add eggs one at a time, beating after each addition. Add vanilla. Combine dry ingredients and add to creamed mixture. Add mashed bananas and mix well. Stir in chocolate chips. Drop by teaspoons onto ungreased cookie sheet. Bake for 12 to 15 minutes. Makes 6 dozen.

Chocolate Chip Breakfast Cookie

1 cup shortening
1 cup sugar
1 cup brown sugar
2 eggs
½ teaspoon vanilla
1 cup flour
1 teaspoon baking soda

1 teaspoon baking powder
1 teaspoon salt
2 cups quick oats
2 cups crisp rice cereal
1 (12 ounce) package
    semisweet chocolate chips

Preheat oven to 350 degrees. Cream shortening, sugars, eggs, and vanilla. Combine flour, baking soda, baking powder, and salt. Add to creamed mixture. Add oats and cereal gradually, stirring lightly after each addition. Bake on lightly greased cookie sheets for about 10 minutes.

Christmas around the World

Suddenly a great company of the heavenly host
appeared with the angel, praising God and saying,
"Glory to God in the highest, and on earth peace
to men on whom his favor rests."

Luke 2:13–14

Viennese Walnut Cookies

½ cup butter
⅓ cup sugar
¼ teaspoon salt
1 teaspoon vanilla
1¼ cups flour
1 cup finely chopped walnuts

Preheat oven to 350 degrees. Cream butter, sugar, salt, and vanilla. Add flour and walnuts. Blend well. Chill for 30 minutes and roll on board to ¼-inch thickness. Cut out cookies using your favorite Christmas shapes. Bake on ungreased sheet for 8 to 10 minutes. Cool and put together by pairs with frosting.

French Butter Cookies

½ cup butter
½ cup vegetable oil
1½ cups powdered sugar
1 egg

1½ teaspoons vanilla
2 cups flour
1 teaspoon cream of tartar
1 teaspoon baking soda

Cream butter, oil, powdered sugar, egg, and vanilla. Beat until thick and creamy. Add dry ingredients. Tint dough with a few drops of red or green food coloring if desired. Chill for at least 2 hours. Shape dough into ¾-inch balls; place on greased cookie sheet about 2 inches apart. Flatten balls with fork and sprinkle with colored sugar. Bake at 350 degrees for 5 to 8 minutes.

Viennese Christmas Tree Cookies

2½ sticks unsalted butter, softened
⅔ cup sugar
2 cups flour
½ cup finely ground almonds

½ finely ground hazelnuts
½ teaspoon cinnamon
1 cup seedless raspberry jam
Powdered sugar

Cream butter and sugar until light and fluffy. Using wooden spoon, beat in flour, almonds, hazelnuts, and cinnamon to make slightly stiff dough. Wrap in plastic wrap and refrigerate for at least 1 hour. Preheat oven to 350 degrees. Lightly grease cookie sheets. Roll out dough to ⅛-inch thickness on lightly floured surface. Cut out Christmas trees with tree-shaped cookie cutter. Place trees on prepared cookie sheets. Using end of drinking straw, make holes in half the trees. Holes will resemble round ornaments when done. Bake for 10 to 12 minutes or until lightly browned. Remove from sheets and cool completely. Spread solid trees with thin layer of raspberry jam. Dust trees with holes with powdered sugar and place on top of jam-coated trees. Makes 3 dozen.

French Lace Cookies

1 cup flour
1 cup finely chopped walnuts
½ cup light corn syrup
½ cup shortening
⅔ cup packed brown sugar

Preheat oven to 375 degrees. Blend flour and nuts. Bring corn syrup, shortening, and sugar to a boil in saucepan over medium heat, stirring constantly. Remove from heat; gradually stir in flour and walnuts. Drop batter by level teaspoons about 3 inches apart on lightly greased baking sheet, baking only 8 cookies at a time. Bake for 5 to 6 minutes; remove from oven and allow to stand for 5 minutes before removing from baking sheet. Makes about 4 dozen.

Russian Tea Cookies

1 cup butter, softened
½ cup powdered sugar
1 teaspoon vanilla
2¼ cups flour
¼ teaspoon salt
½ cup chopped pecans
Additional powdered sugar

Cream butter, powdered sugar, and vanilla. Add flour, salt, and pecans. Cover and chill until firm. Preheat oven to 400 degrees. Roll into balls. Bake just until set, about 8 to 10 minutes. While cookies are still warm, roll in powdered sugar. Store in airtight container.

Old English Cookies

1 cup shortening
2 cups brown sugar
3 eggs
4 cups flour
1 teaspoon baking soda
1 teaspoon baking powder
½ teaspoon salt
½ teaspoon cinnamon

½ teaspoon nutmeg
1 cup brewed cold coffee
½ teaspoon vanilla
1 cup chopped walnuts
1 cup raisins
1 cup semisweet
   chocolate chips

Preheat oven to 350 degrees. Grease cookie sheets. Cream shortening and brown sugar. Add eggs one at a time, beating well until light and fluffy. Add dry ingredients alternately with coffee. Beat well. Mix in vanilla, walnuts, raisins, and chocolate chips. Drop cookies by tablespoons onto prepared cookie sheets. Bake for 15 minutes; cool on wire rack.

English Christmas Cookies

⅔ cup shortening
2 cups brown sugar
3 eggs
2½ cups flour, divided
3 teaspoons baking powder
1 teaspoon salt

½ teaspoon cinnamon
½ teaspoon nutmeg
½ teaspoon cloves
⅔ cup milk
1 cup raisins
1 cup chopped pecans

Preheat oven to 350 degrees. Cream shortening, adding brown sugar gradually. Beat eggs very lightly and add to creamed mixture. Sift 2 cups flour with baking powder, salt, and spices. Add alternately with milk. Add raisins and pecans and enough extra flour to make stiff dough. Drop by teaspoons onto greased baking sheet. Bake for 8 to 10 minutes or until golden brown.

Chinese New Year Cookies

½ cup semisweet chocolate chips
½ cup butterscotch chips
1 (3 ounce) can chow mein noodles
1 (7 ounce) can salted peanuts

Heat chocolate and butterscotch chips in microwave for 1 minute on high. Stir. Continue heating for 30 seconds at a time until chips are smooth. Mix in noodles and peanuts. Drop by teaspoons onto wax paper. Chill. Makes about 4 dozen.

Swedish Shortbread Cookies

1 pound butter
1½ cups sugar
1 teaspoon orange extract
1 egg
Zest of 1 orange and 1 lemon

¾ teaspoon salt
5 cups flour
Candied cherries
Chopped nuts

Preheat oven to 350 degrees. Cream butter and sugar. Add orange extract, egg, zest, and salt. Add flour a little at a time. Drop by teaspoons onto ungreased baking sheet. To decorate, press candied cherry in center and roll edges in chopped nuts. Bake for 8 to 10 minutes.

Swedish Ginger Cookies

⅓ cup brown sugar
⅓ cup molasses
1 teaspoon ginger
½ teaspoon cinnamon
¼ teaspoon cloves
2¼ teaspoons baking soda
⅓ cup butter
1 egg
2½ cups flour

Frosting:
1 egg white
¼ teaspoon cream of tartar
Powdered sugar

Heat brown sugar, molasses, and spices together to boiling. Remove from heat and add baking soda; add butter and stir until melted. Add egg and beat well; then stir in almost all the flour. Place remaining flour on kneading board, put dough on top, and knead until flour is absorbed. Roll dough very thin, cut into shapes, and bake at 350 degrees for about 5 minutes. Frost.

Swedish Coconut Cookies

1 cup shortening
1 cup butter
2 cups sugar
3 cups flour
1 teaspoon baking soda
1 teaspoon baking powder
1 cup flaked coconut, toasted
1 teaspoon vanilla

Preheat oven to 350 degrees. Cream shortening, butter, and sugar. Add dry ingredients, coconut, and vanilla. Shape into balls. Press with bottom of glass dipped in sugar. Bake for 7 to 8 minutes.

Swedish Butter Cookies

2 sticks butter (no substitutions)   Dash salt
1 cup sugar   Nuts
1 teaspoon vanilla   Candied cherries
2 cups flour   Chocolate chips
1 teaspoon baking powder

Preheat oven to 300 degrees. Cream butter and sugar and beat until fluffy. Add vanilla; stir in flour sifted with baking powder and salt. Mix until smooth. Form into small balls; place on ungreased baking sheet. Press nut, cherry, or chocolate chip on top of each. Bake for 20 minutes or until edges are lightly browned.

Irish Drop Cookies

1½ cups raisins
1 cup hot water
⅔ cup shortening
1 cup sugar
1 cup brown sugar
2 eggs

3½ cups flour
½ teaspoon salt
½ teaspoon cinnamon
½ teaspoon nutmeg
1 teaspoon baking soda

Preheat oven to 375 degrees. Simmer raisins in hot water for 15 minutes. Drain and reserve ½ cup liquid. Mix shortening, sugars, and eggs. Sift flour, salt, and spices. Add baking soda to reserved liquid and mix with shortening mixture. Blend in flour mixture. Mix well. Drop on baking sheet. Bake for 10 to 12 minutes.

Irish Lace Cookies

1 stick unsalted butter, softened
¾ cup packed light brown sugar
2 tablespoons flour
2 tablespoons whole milk

1 teaspoon vanilla
Pinch cinnamon
1¼ cups old-fashioned
   rolled oats

Preheat oven to 350 degrees. Cream butter and brown sugar until light and fluffy. Beat in flour, milk, vanilla, and cinnamon. Stir in oats. Drop dough by rounded teaspoons about 3 inches apart on ungreased baking sheets. Bake for 10 to 12 minutes or until golden. Let stand on sheets for 1 minute. Transfer to wire rack and cool completely. Makes about 40 cookies.

Mexican Yuletide Cookies

1 cup butter, softened
¾ cup powdered sugar
1 teaspoon vanilla
2 cups flour
1 cup rolled oats
1 cup chopped walnuts
Additional powdered sugar

Preheat oven to 325 degrees. Beat butter until creamy. Add powdered sugar; continue to beat. Add vanilla and flour. Blend well. Stir in oats and walnuts; mix well. Shape into balls and bake for 20 to 25 minutes. Sprinkle with powdered sugar while cookies are still warm.

Spanish Peanut Cookies

1 cup shortening
1 cup sugar
1 cup brown sugar
2 eggs
½ teaspoon vanilla

1 teaspoon baking soda
1½ cups flour
3 cups rolled oats
½ pound Spanish peanuts

Preheat oven to 400 degrees. Cream shortening and sugars. Add eggs and vanilla. Add baking soda and flour. Stir in rolled oats and peanuts. Form into small balls. Bake for 10 to 15 minutes. Makes about 7 dozen.

Mexican Wedding Cookies

1 cup butter
½ cup sugar
2 teaspoons vanilla
2 teaspoons water

2 cups flour
1 cup chopped almonds
½ cup powdered sugar

Cream butter and sugar. Stir in vanilla and water. Add flour and almonds. Mix until well blended. Wrap dough tightly in plastic wrap and chill for at least 3 hours. Preheat oven to 325 degrees. Shape dough into balls or crescents. Place on ungreased cookie sheet and bake for 15 to 20 minutes. Remove from sheet to cool on wire racks. When cool, roll in powdered sugar. Store at room temperature in airtight container.

Chinese Almond Cookies

1 cup shortening
½ cup sugar
¼ cup packed brown sugar
1 egg
1 teaspoon almond extract
2¼ cups flour

⅛ teaspoon salt
1½ teaspoons baking powder
5 dozen whole blanched
    almonds
1 egg yolk
2 tablespoons water

Preheat oven to 350 degrees. In large bowl with electric mixer, beat shortening and sugars until creamy. Add whole egg and almond extract; beat until well blended. In another bowl, stir together flour, salt, and baking powder; add to creamed mixture, blending thoroughly. To shape each cookie, roll about 1 tablespoon dough into ball. Place balls 2 inches apart on ungreased baking sheets then flatten each slightly to make 2-inch circle. Gently press almond into center of each round. Place egg yolk and water in small bowl; beat together lightly with fork. Brush mixture over top of each cookie with pastry brush. Bake for 10 to 12 minutes or until lightly browned. Transfer to wire rack and cool. Store in airtight container.

English Scones for Christmas

2 cups flour
½ cup sugar
1½ teaspoons baking powder
1 teaspoon baking soda
¼ teaspoon salt
½ cup butter, very cold
1 egg

1 teaspoon vanilla
½ cup minus 2 tablespoons
  buttermilk
1 cup chopped dried
  cranberries
½ cup chopped walnuts

Mix dry ingredients well. Cut in butter until mixture resembles coarse pebbles. Beat egg, vanilla, and buttermilk; add to dry ingredients. Mix briefly. Add cranberries and walnuts; mix. Turn dough out on well-floured cutting board. Knead briefly, working in enough flour to make stiff dough. Shape into rectangle about 1½ inches thick. Cut into 12 squares. Bake at 400 degrees for 20 minutes. Makes about 1 dozen.

Healthy and Wonderful

Love came down at Christmas,
Love all lovely, love divine;
Love was born at Christmas,
Star and angels gave the sign.

Christina Georgina Rossetti

Healthy Oatmeal Cookies

2 cups brown sugar
3 cups wheat flour
2 teaspoons salt
2 teaspoons baking soda
1 teaspoon baking powder

6 cups rolled oats
2 cups applesauce
2 eggs
2 teaspoons vanilla

Mix dry ingredients. Add applesauce, eggs, and vanilla. Mix well. Drop by teaspoons onto greased baking sheet. Bake at 350 degrees for 10 to 12 minutes.

Oatmeal Pumpkin Cookies

1 cup pumpkin
2 egg whites, whipped
1 cup packed brown sugar
1½ cups flour
1 teaspoon baking soda

1 teaspoon cinnamon
½ teaspoon nutmeg
½ teaspoon cloves
3 cups rolled oats

Preheat oven to 350. Spray baking sheet with cooking spray. In large bowl, combine pumpkin and egg whites. In separate bowl, combine brown sugar, flour, baking soda, cinnamon, nutmeg, cloves, and oats. Mix ingredients together just until moistened. Drop cookies by tablespoons onto prepared baking sheet. Bake for 15 minutes.

Healthy Oatmeal Chocolate Chip Cookies

½ cup butter
1¾ cup brown sugar
2 cups wheat flour
1 teaspoon baking soda
1 teaspoon salt
2½ cups quick oats

½ cup applesauce
2 eggs
¼ cup milk
1 teaspoon vanilla
1 cup semisweet chocolate chips

Cream butter and brown sugar. Add dry ingredients. Add applesauce, eggs, milk, and vanilla. Mix well. Stir in chocolate chips. Drop by teaspoons onto greased baking sheet. Bake at 350 degrees for 10 to 12 minutes.

Nutritious No-Bake Cookies

½ cup peanut butter
½ cup honey or corn syrup
¼ cup orange juice
1½ cups nonfat dry milk

Mix all ingredients thoroughly. Add 4 cups crisp rice cereal. Mix. Shape into small balls. Makes about 4 dozen.

Tasty Wheat Germ Cookies

1 box yellow cake mix
1 egg
3 tablespoons brown sugar
¼ cup vegetable oil
2 tablespoons butter, melted
½ cup wheat germ
2 tablespoons water
½ cup chopped peanuts

Preheat oven to 375 degrees. Combine dry cake mix, egg, brown sugar, oil, butter, wheat germ, and water. Add peanuts; mix well. Drop by teaspoons onto ungreased cookie sheets. Bake for 10 minutes for chewy cookies or 12 minutes for crispy cookies. Cool for 1 minute and remove from sheet.

Chocolate Oatmeal Raisin Cookies

½ cup white flour
½ cup wheat flour
½ teaspoon baking powder
¼ cup vegetable oil
¼ cup skim milk
½ cup crushed pineapple
1 teaspoon lemon juice

1 teaspoon vanilla
1 teaspoon cinnamon
2 cups oatmeal
¾ cup raisins
¼ cup semisweet
  chocolate chips

Preheat oven to 350 degrees. Mix all ingredients together. Drop by teaspoons onto ungreased cookie sheet. Bake for 20 minutes.

Amazing Apple Butter Cookies

1 cup sugar
1 cup butter, softened
¼ cup apple butter
1 egg

2½ cups flour
1 cup shredded cheddar cheese
½ teaspoon baking soda
½ teaspoon cinnamon

Preheat oven to 400 degrees. Mix sugar, butter, apple butter, and egg; stir in remaining ingredients. Cover and refrigerate for 2 hours. Divide dough in half. Shape each half into 8-inch-long roll. Wrap and refrigerate for at least 4 hours. Cut rolls into ⅛-inch slices. Place on ungreased cookie sheet. Bake for 7 to 9 minutes.

Lip-Smacking Banana Split Cookies

½ cup butter
1 cup packed brown sugar
2 eggs
1 cup mashed bananas
2 cups flour
2 teaspoons baking powder

¼ teaspoon baking soda
¼ teaspoon salt
½ teaspoon cinnamon
¼ teaspoon cloves
½ cup chopped peanuts

Preheat oven to 375 degrees. Cream butter and brown sugar. Beat in eggs and bananas. Sift together flour, baking powder, baking soda, salt, cinnamon, and cloves; blend into banana mixture. Stir in peanuts. Cover and chill for at least 1 hour. Drop dough by rounded teaspoons onto lightly greased cookie sheet. Bake for 8 to 10 minutes.

Banana Chocolate Chip Oatmeal Cookies

2 cups mashed bananas
4 cups quick oats
½ teaspoon vanilla
⅔ cup semisweet chocolate chips
½ cup applesauce
½ teaspoon cinnamon

Preheat oven to 350 degrees. Mix all ingredients together until moist. Drop dough by tablespoonfuls on an ungreased cookie sheet. Flatten to desired thickness. Bake for 15 minutes. Store in airtight container.

Healthy Gingerbread Cookies

2¼ cups whole wheat flour
½ tablespoon baking soda
1 teaspoon ginger
½ cup molasses
⅓ cup orange juice
Dash cinnamon

Preheat oven to 300 degrees. Mix flour, baking soda, and ginger. Add molasses, orange juice, and cinnamon. Mix well. Form into 1-inch balls. Place on greased cookie sheet. Flatten to desired thickness. Bake for 10 minutes or until firm.

Cranberry Drop Cookies

½ cup butter
1 cup sugar
¾ cup packed brown sugar
¼ cup milk
2 tablespoons orange juice
1 egg
3 cups flour
1 teaspoon baking powder

½ teaspoon cinnamon
½ teaspoon salt
¼ teaspoon baking soda
1 cup chopped walnuts
   or pecans
2½ cups chopped fresh
   cranberries

Preheat oven to 375 degrees. Cream butter and sugars. Beat in milk, orange juice, and egg. Combine flour, baking powder, cinnamon, salt, and baking soda. Blend well with sugar mixture. Stir in nuts and cranberries. Drop dough by teaspoons onto greased cookie sheet. Bake for 10 to 15 minutes or until lightly browned. Makes about 7 dozen.

Feel Good Chocolate Chip Balls

1 cup margarine
½ cup sugar substitute
¼ cup egg substitute
1½ teaspoons vanilla
3 cups whole wheat flour

½ cup oat bran
1¼ teaspoons baking
  powder
1 cup chocolate or
  carob chips

Preheat oven to 375 degrees. Blend margarine and sugar until fluffy. Add egg and vanilla; mix just until combined. Gradually add flour, bran, and baking powder. Stir in chocolate or carob chips. Shape into balls and place on ungreased cookie sheet. Bake for 10 minutes or until lightly browned. Remove from oven, let cool for 1 minute, and remove from cookie sheet.

Winter Trail Mix Cookies

2 medium bananas, mashed
½ cup molasses
¼ cup honey
1 tablespoon cornstarch
½ cup applesauce
¼ cup water
1 teaspoon vanilla
1 cup whole wheat flour

1 teaspoon cinnamon
½ teaspoon baking soda
½ teaspoon cloves
½ cup raisins
½ cup semisweet chocolate chips
½ cup peanuts
3 cups quick oats

Preheat oven to 350 degrees. Mix bananas, molasses, honey, cornstarch, applesauce, water, and vanilla. Stir in flour, cinnamon, baking soda, and cloves. Add raisins, chocolate chips, peanuts, and oats. Dough will be very heavy. Form into 16 balls; flatten and shape into large, round cookies. Bake for 12 to 15 minutes on lightly greased cookie sheet.

Cake Mix Cookies

Good news from heaven the angels bring,
Glad tidings to the earth they sing:
To us this day a child is given,
To crown us with the joy of heaven.

MARTIN LUTHER

German Chocolate Cookies

1 box German chocolate cake mix
1 stick margarine, softened
2 eggs, beaten
1 cup shredded coconut, divided

24 chocolate-covered soft
    caramel candies
1 tub chocolate fudge frosting
½ cup crushed pecans (optional)

Preheat oven to 350 degrees. Mix cake mix, margarine, eggs, and ½ cup coconut until well blended. Pinch off small amount of dough and form ball. Push caramel candy into center and roll to reform ball shape. Place on greased cookie sheet. Bake for 8 to 10 minutes. Remove from oven and let set. When cookies are cool, frost with chocolate fudge frosting then sprinkle with remaining coconut and pecans (optional). Makes 2 dozen.

Triple Chip Wonder Cookies

1 box white cake mix
1 stick butter or margarine, melted
2 eggs
½ cup white chocolate chips
½ cup butterscotch chips
½ cup semisweet chocolate chips

Mix cake mix with melted butter and eggs. Stir in chips. Drop spoonfuls onto ungreased cookie sheet. Bake for 6 to 7 minutes at 350 degrees. Do not overbake; cookies will set up as they cool.

Lazy Lemon Cookies

1 box lemon cake mix
1 stick butter or margarine, melted
2 eggs
2 cups white chocolate chips

Preheat oven to 350 degrees. Mix cake mix, butter, and eggs until dough forms. Stir in chocolate chips. Drop spoonfuls onto ungreased cookie sheet. Bake for 8 to 10 minutes. Let cool and store in airtight container.

Butter Pecan Cookies

1 box butter pecan cake mix
1 (9 ounce) package pecan pieces
2 eggs
1 stick butter, softened

Preheat oven to 350 degrees. Beat butter and eggs. Add cake mix and pecans. Mix well. Batter will be stiff. Drop spoonfuls onto ungreased cookie sheet. Bake for 10 to 12 minutes. Makes 3 to 4 dozen.

Chocolate Crinkles

1 box chocolate cake mix
1 large egg
¼ cup oil
¼ cup water
1 cup semisweet chocolate chips
2 cups powdered sugar

Preheat oven to 350 degrees. Combine cake mix, egg, oil, and water. Beat until well blended. Stir in chocolate chips. Shape into balls and roll in powdered sugar. Place about 1 inch apart on greased cookie sheet. Bake for 12 to 15 minutes. Sprinkle with additional powdered sugar.

Easy Cake Mix Cookies

1 box cake mix (any flavor)
1 large egg
¼ cup oil
¼ cup water
1 cup any or all of the following: chopped nuts, raisins, oatmeal, coconut,
    chocolate chips, or candy-coated chocolate pieces

Preheat oven to 350 degrees. Combine cake mix, egg, oil, and water. Beat until well blended. Stir in remaining ingredient(s). Drop by teaspoons about 1 inch apart on greased cookie sheet. Bake for 12 to 15 minutes or until done.

Crispy Cake Mix Cookies

1 box chocolate cake mix
1 cup crisp rice cereal
½ cup butter, melted
1 egg, slightly beaten
¼ cup semisweet chocolate chips

Preheat oven to 350 degrees. Blend all ingredients. Form into 1-inch balls and place on ungreased cookie sheet. Bake for 9 to 13 minutes.

Cake Mix Cutout Cookies

1 box yellow cake mix
2 eggs
¼ cup vegetable oil
½ cup sugar
Frosting and holiday decorations

Preheat oven to 350 degrees. Mix all ingredients. Roll out small amounts of dough on pastry sheets. Cut with cookie cutters. Place on cookie sheet. Bake for 5 to 10 minutes. Cool and decorate.

Peanut Butter Chocolate Chip Cake Mix Cookies

2 eggs
⅓ cup water
¼ cup butter, softened
1 cup peanut butter
1 box white cake mix
1 (12 ounce) package semisweet chocolate chips

Preheat oven to 375 degrees. Beat eggs, water, butter, peanut butter, and half the cake mix with electric mixer until light and fluffy. Stir in remaining cake mix and chocolate chips. Drop by rounded teaspoons on ungreased baking sheet. Bake for 10 to 12 minutes.

Simple Snickerdoodle Cookies

1 box cinnamon swirl cake mix
2 eggs
1 stick butter or margarine

Preheat oven to 350 degrees. Mix cake mix, eggs, and butter until dough forms. Place cinnamon mixture from box in bowl. Shape dough into small balls; roll in cinnamon mixture and place on ungreased cookie sheet. Bake for 8 to 10 minutes. For softer cookies, leave slightly underbaked and let set. Store in airtight container.

Holiday Bar Cookies

Ring out the old, ring in the new,
Ring, happy bells, across the snow:
The year is going, let him go;
Ring out the false, ring in the true.

ALFRED, LORD TENNYSON

Chocolate Candy Caramel Bars

1 box chocolate cake mix with pudding
½ cup shortening
1 cup evaporated milk, divided
1 package soft caramels
1 (14 ounce) bag candy-coated chocolate pieces

Preheat oven to 350 degrees. Grease 9x12-inch pan. Combine cake mix, shortening, and ⅔ cup evaporated milk. Mix well. Spread half the batter in pan. Bake for 15 minutes. Combine caramels and ⅓ cup evaporated milk and heat in microwave until smooth. Sprinkle 1 cup candy-coated chocolate pieces over batter. Drizzle with caramel mixture. Spoon remaining batter over caramel. Add remaining candy-coated chocolate pieces. Bake for 25 minutes. Cool. Cut into bars.

Magic Nutty Bars

½ cup butter
1½ cups graham cracker crumbs
1 (14 ounce) can sweetened condensed milk
1 (6 ounce) package semisweet chocolate chips
1⅓ cups flaked coconut
1 cup chopped pecans or peanuts

Preheat oven to 350 degrees. Melt butter in 9x13-inch pan. Sprinkle crumbs evenly over melted butter; pour sweetened condensed milk evenly over crumbs. Top evenly with remaining ingredients; press down firmly with fork. Bake for 25 minutes or until lightly browned. Cool and cut into bars.

Chocolate Cheesecake Cookie Bars

2 tubes refrigerated chocolate chip cookie dough
1 (12 ounce) package milk chocolate chips
2 (8 ounce) packages cream cheese
2 eggs
1 teaspoon vanilla

Preheat oven to 350 degrees. Grease 9x13-inch pan. Press 1 tube of cookie dough evenly into pan, forming crust. Melt chocolate chips in microwave for 30 seconds. Stir. Repeat until creamy. Blend cream cheese, eggs, and vanilla until smooth. Fold in melted chocolate. Layer over dough in pan. Cut second tube of cookie dough in ¼-inch slices. Place on top of chocolate cream cheese mixture. Cover completely to form top crust. Bake for 30 minutes. Chill and refrigerate or freeze before serving.

Caramel Chocolate Pecan Bars

1 cup flour
1 cup quick oats
½ teaspoon baking soda
¼ teaspoon salt
¾ cup sugar

¾ cup butter
1 (14 ounce) package caramels
⅓ cup evaporated milk
½ cup chopped pecans
1 cup chocolate semisweet chips

Preheat oven to 350 degrees. Combine flour, oats, baking soda, and salt. Beat in butter and sugar until fluffy. Beat in oat mixture until crumbly. Do not overmix (you may need another ½ cup or so of oats to make mixture crumbly). Reserve 1 cup crust mixture and press remainder in ungreased 9x13-inch pan. Bake for 10 minutes. Cool in pan for 10 minutes. In saucepan, cook caramels and evaporated milk over low heat until caramels melt and mixture is smooth. Spread over baked cookie crust. Sprinkle with pecans then with reserved crumbs and chocolate chips. Bake for 15 to 20 minutes or until top crumbs are golden. Cool in pan on wire rack. Cut into bars. Makes 32.

Zucchini Carrot Cookie Bars

⅔ cup brown sugar
½ cup butter
1 egg
1 teaspoon vanilla
½ cup flour
1 teaspoon baking powder
½ teaspoon salt
½ teaspoon cinnamon
⅔ cup grated carrot
⅔ cup grated zucchini
½ cup raisins
3 ounces cream cheese, softened

Frosting:

¼ cup butter
3 ounces cream cheese, softened
½ cup powdered sugar
½ teaspoon vanilla
Colored sugar

Beat together all ingredients. Spoon into greased 9x9-inch pan. Bake at 350 degrees for 30 minutes. Cool for 10 minutes. Frost when cool. Makes 12. **Frosting:** Beat together butter and cream cheese. Add powdered sugar and vanilla. Beat until creamy and smooth. Spread on bars and decorate with colored sugars.

Chocolate Cookie Bars

2 cups finely crushed chocolate sandwich cookies
¼ cup butter, melted
1 (12 ounce) package semisweet chocolate chips
1 (14 ounce) can sweetened condensed milk
1 teaspoon vanilla

Preheat oven to 350 degrees. Combine crushed cookies and butter; press firmly on bottom of 9x13-inch baking pan. In medium saucepan over medium heat, melt 1 cup chocolate chips with condensed milk and vanilla. Pour evenly over crust mix and sprinkle with remaining chips. Bake for 20 minutes or until set. Cool. Cut into bars. Store tightly covered at room temperature.

Double Fudge Nut Bars

1¾ cups flour
¾ cup powdered sugar
¼ cup cocoa
1 cup cold butter
1 (12 ounce) package semisweet
   chocolate chips

1 (14 ounce) can sweetened
   condensed milk
1 teaspoon vanilla
1 cup chopped walnuts

Preheat oven to 350 degrees. Mix flour, powdered sugar, and cocoa. Cut in cold butter. Press into 9x13-inch pan. Bake for 15 minutes. Melt 1 cup chocolate chips in saucepan with condensed milk and vanilla. When melted, pour over crust. Sprinkle with remaining chocolate chips and walnuts. Press down lightly. Bake for 20 minutes.

Almond Roca Bars

1 cup butter
½ cup sugar
½ cup brown sugar
1 egg, beaten
1 teaspoon vanilla
½ teaspoon almond extract

2 cups minus 2 tablespoons
  flour
1 (12 ounce) bag semisweet
  chocolate chips
1 small package slivered or
  roasted almonds

Preheat oven to 350 degrees. Cream butter and sugars. Add remaining ingredients except chocolate chips and almonds. Mix thoroughly and spread on large cookie sheet. Bake for 10 to 12 minutes. Melt chocolate chips in microwave for 30 seconds. Stir. Repeat until creamy. Spread over warm cookie and sprinkle slivered almonds on top. Cut into bars when cool.

Lemon Pie Cookie Bars

1⅓ cups plus 2 tablespoons flour, divided
1 cup sugar, divided
½ cup butter, softened
2 eggs
¼ teaspoon baking powder

Juice and zest of
   1 large lemon
Powdered sugar or
   whipped cream

Preheat oven to 350 degrees. Combine 1⅓ cups flour, ¼ cup sugar, and butter. Press into greased 8x8-inch pan. Bake for 15 to 20 minutes or until edges are brown. Combine 2 tablespoons flour, ¾ sugar, eggs, baking powder, and lemon juice and zest. Mix well. Pour over crust and continue baking for 18 minutes or until set. Remove from oven and sprinkle with powdered sugar, or cool and top with whipped cream. Cut into bars after cooling.

Raspberry Oatmeal Bars

½ cup butter, softened
½ cup brown sugar
1 cup flour
¼ teaspoon baking soda
⅛ teaspoon salt
1 cup quick oats
¾ cup seedless raspberry jam

Preheat oven to 350 degrees. Mix all ingredients together except jam. Press 2 cups mixture into bottom of greased 8x8-inch pan. Spread jam to within ¼ inch of edge. Sprinkle remaining crumb mixture over top and press down lightly. Bake for 35 to 40 minutes. Allow to cool before cutting into bars.

Noel Bars

2 eggs, beaten
1 cup brown sugar
5 tablespoons flour
⅛ teaspoon baking soda
1 cup chopped pecans

1 teaspoon vanilla
2 tablespoons butter, melted
Pinch cinnamon
Powdered sugar

Preheat oven to 350 degrees. Mix together eggs, brown sugar, flour, baking soda, pecans, and vanilla. Pour melted butter into 7x11-inch pan. Top with cinnamon. Pour batter over melted butter and cinnamon without stirring. Bake for 20 minutes. Cool, cut into squares, and sprinkle with powdered sugar.

Raisin Spice Bars

1 cup raisins
1 cup water
½ cup vegetable oil
1 cup sugar
1 egg, slightly beaten
1¾ cups flour
1 teaspoon baking soda
¼ teaspoon salt

1 teaspoon cinnamon
½ teaspoon nutmeg
½ teaspoon allspice
Dash cloves
½ cup chopped pecans or
　walnuts
¼ cup powdered sugar

Preheat oven to 375 degrees. Combine raisins and water in medium saucepan; bring to a boil. Remove from heat and stir in oil; allow to cool to lukewarm. Stir in sugar and beaten egg. Sift together dry ingredients; beat into raisin mixture with wooden spoon. Stir in chopped nuts. Pour into greased and floured 9x13-inch pan. Bake for 18 to 24 minutes. Cool in pan then cut into bars. Sprinkle with powdered sugar.

Festive Chocolate Mint Bars

2 eggs, beaten
½ cup butter or margarine, melted
1 cup sugar
2 ounces semisweet chocolate chips
½ teaspoon peppermint extract
½ cup flour

Frosting:
2 tablespoons butter, softened
1 tablespoon heavy whipping cream
1 cup powdered sugar
1 teaspoon peppermint extract
Red or green food coloring
1 ounce semisweet chocolate chips, melted

Preheat oven to 350 degrees. Cream eggs, melted butter, and sugar. Melt chocolate chips in microwave for 30 seconds. Stir. Repeat until creamy. Add melted chocolate and peppermint extract to creamed mixture; stir until well blended. Stir in flour and blend well. Pour into greased and floured 9x9-inch pan. Bake for 25 to 30 minutes. **Frosting:** Thoroughly blend butter and cream; add powdered sugar, peppermint extract, and food coloring. Spread over cooled chocolate peppermint bars. Melt chocolate chips in microwave for 30 seconds. Stir. Repeat until creamy. When frosting is firm, spread melted chocolate over top. Place in refrigerator until topping is firm. Cut into small bars.

Ginger Cream Bars

1 cup sugar
1 cup butter, softened
2 cups flour
1 teaspoon salt
2 teaspoons baking soda
1 tablespoon cinnamon
1 tablespoon ginger
1 teaspoon cloves
2 eggs
½ cup molasses
1 cup hot coffee

Frosting:

½ cup butter, softened
3 ounces cream cheese, softened
2 cups powdered sugar
2 teaspoons vanilla

Preheat oven to 350 degrees. Cream sugar and butter. Sift together flour, salt, baking soda, and spices; add to creamed mixture. Add eggs one at a time, beating well after each addition. Blend in molasses then coffee. Spread in 10x15-inch pan. Bake for 20 to 25 minutes. Cool. **Frosting:** Cream butter and cream cheese; add powdered sugar and vanilla and beat until fluffy. Spread over bars.

Marshmallow Mud Bars

2 cups sugar
1 cup shortening
4 eggs
2½ teaspoons vanilla
1½ cups flour
⅓ cup cocoa
⅓ teaspoon salt
1 (6½ ounce) bag mini marshmallows

Frosting:
    2 sticks butter, softened
    ½ cup cocoa
    1 box powdered sugar
    1 teaspoon vanilla
    ½ cup evaporated milk

Preheat oven to 300 degrees. Cream sugar and shortening. Add eggs and vanilla. Sift flour, cocoa, and salt together. Add to creamed mixture and beat until well combined. Pour mixture into greased and floured 9x13-inch glass baking dish. Bake for 35 minutes. **Frosting:** While bars are baking, beat together the butter, cocoa, powdered sugar, and vanilla. Slowly add evaporated milk. Set aside. After baking bars, remove from oven and spread marshmallows on top. Return to oven for 5 more minutes. Allow to cool completely. Frost bars and let stand for about 2 hours before cutting into squares.

Rich Brownie Bars

4 squares unsweetened baking chocolate
1 cup butter
2 cups sugar
1 cup flour
4 eggs, beaten

2 teaspoons hot coffee
1 cup semisweet chocolate
   chips
1 cup chopped nuts

Preheat oven to 325 degrees. Grease 9x13-inch baking pan. In small saucepan over low heat, melt chocolate and butter, stirring constantly. Remove from heat. In large bowl, combine sugar and flour. Add chocolate mixture, eggs, and coffee; stir until well blended. Stir in chocolate chips and nuts. Spread batter into prepared pan. Bake for 35 minutes. Cool completely before cutting. Refrigerate for at least 2 hours before serving.

Easy Chocolate Pizza Bars

1 tube refrigerated chocolate chip cookie dough
½ cup peanut butter
1 cup milk chocolate chips
Assorted candy bars and holiday decorations

Press cookie dough into round pizza pan or 9x13-inch pan and bake as directed. Immediately after removing from oven, drop peanut butter onto pizza. Sprinkle chocolate chips on top. Wait about 2 minutes until peanut butter and chocolate chips begin to melt; then spread. Chop up assorted candy bars and sprinkle on top. Decorate with holiday sprinkles and cut into bars.

White Chocolate Wonder Bars

1½ cups flour
½ teaspoon baking powder
⅛ teaspoon salt
10 teaspoons unsalted butter
12 ounces white chocolate chips
¾ cups sugar
3 eggs
3 teaspoons vanilla
4 ounces semisweet chocolate chips
¾ cup chopped macadamia nuts, toasted

Preheat oven to 325 degrees. Grease 9x9-inch pan. Line bottom of pan with parchment paper and set aside. Sift together flour, baking powder, and salt. Melt butter in small saucepan. Do not allow butter to bubble or brown. Remove from heat and add half the white chocolate chips. Do not stir chocolate; just set aside for about 5 minutes. Beat sugar, eggs, and vanilla for about 5 minutes until thick and lemon colored. Add butter mixture. Mix just until blended. Add flour mixture and mix just until flour is mixed in. Use rubber spatula to fold in all the chocolate—the white chocolate chips melted with butter and the remaining white chocolate and semisweet chocolate chips—and the nuts. Spread batter in prepared pan. Bake for 30 minutes or until bars are just set. Do not overbake. Allow to cool for 1 hour; then cut into squares.

Chocolate Truffle Bars

1 cup sugar
½ cup butter, softened
1 teaspoon vanilla
2 eggs
⅔ cup flour
½ cup cocoa
½ teaspoon baking powder
½ teaspoon salt
½ cup chopped walnuts

Truffle topping:
4 (2 ounce) dark chocolate bars
¾ cup whipping cream
1 tablespoon light corn syrup
1 tablespoon unsalted
  butter, softened

Preheat oven to 350 degrees. Mix sugar, butter, vanilla, and eggs. Stir in remaining ingredients. Spread in greased 8x8-inch pan. Bake for 25 to 30 minutes. Cool completely before adding topping. **Truffle topping:** Chop chocolate bars and melt in microwave or in double boiler. In separate saucepan, combine cream and corn syrup and bring to a boil. Pour hot corn syrup mixture over melted chocolate and whisk to completely combine. Allow chocolate mixture to cool for 5 minutes. Whisk softened butter into chocolate mixture. Allow to cool to room temperature. Mixture will have thick, custard-like consistency. Whisk until mixture begins to lighten in color slightly. Spread evenly over cooled bars. Allow bars to stand at room temperature until topping firms up. Dust lightly with cocoa if desired. Cut into bars. Store in airtight container.

Frosted Apple Bars

½ cup lukewarm milk
2 eggs
2 teaspoons instant yeast
4 cups flour
1 teaspoon salt
1 cup unsalted butter,
   cut into chunks

Glaze:
   1 cup powdered sugar
   2 tablespoons milk
   1 teaspoon vanilla

Filling:
   ¾ cup sugar
   ¼ cup cornstarch
   ¼ teaspoon salt
   2 teaspoons cinnamon
   8 cups Granny Smith apples

Beat milk and eggs together and set aside. Combine yeast, flour, and salt; cut in butter with pastry blender or two knives until mixture resembles coarse crumbs. Add egg mixture, stirring until soft dough forms. Divide dough in half, wrap in plastic wrap, and refrigerate for about 30 minutes. **Filling:** Lightly grease 13x18-inch pan. Combine sugar, cornstarch, salt, and cinnamon; set aside. On lightly floured surface, roll half the dough into very thin rectangle a little smaller than size of pan. Transfer dough to prepared pan. Peel and core apples and slice very thin. Spread apples over dough and sprinkle with sugar mixture. Roll out remaining dough and place on top of apples. Pinch edges together. Cut steam vents in top. Cover with plastic wrap lightly coated with cooking spray and let rise in a cool place for about 1 hour. Bake for 25 to 30 minutes at 350 degrees. Cool on wire rack for 20 minutes; then drizzle with prepared glaze. **Glaze:** Combine all glaze ingredients until smooth. Let bars cool completely and cut into squares. Refrigerate any leftovers.

INDEX